Mother Goose Math

BY DEBORAH SCHECTER

SCHOLASTIC
PROFESSIONALBOOKS

NEW YORK • TORONTO • LONDON • AUCKLAND • SYDNEY
MEXICO CITY • NEW DELHI • HONG KONG • BUENOS AIRES

For my sister,
Gail

Front cover and interior design by Kathy Massaro
Cover photographs by James Levin
Cover and interior illustrations by Maxie Chambliss

ISBN: 0-439-15584-3
Copyright © 2003 by Deborah Schecter.
Published by Scholastic Inc.
All rights reserved.
Printed in the U. S. A.

6 7 8 9 10   40   09 08 07 06 05 04 03

Contents

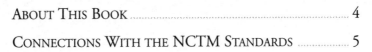

NURSERY RHYME	MATH FOCUS	PAGE

About This Book

Teaching Math With Mother Goose

"One, Two, Buckle My Shoe"…"Old Mother Hubbard"…"Simple Simon"…these and other beloved nursery rhymes have delighted children for generations. Rhythmic and playful, and filled with a myriad of math connections, nursery rhymes are a natural motivator for teaching math skills and concepts to young children. Each of the nursery rhymes included in this book forms the basis for a lesson on one or more key math skills or concepts. The fun-filled activities, games, and manipulatives are inviting ways to help children practice counting, adding and subtracting, patterning, classifying, and more. So get ready to see rhyme-rich math in action as children add and subtract The Queen of Hearts' tarts, measure a flower growing in Mistress Mary's garden, and help Little Bo-Peep find her lost sheep using simple coordinate geometry!

Whether the children in your class are familiar with these timeless verses or are experiencing them for the first time, the nursery rhymes and activities in *Mother Goose Math* are sure to spark smiles and laughter and foster a love of math!

What's Inside

Each ready-to-reproduce nursery rhyme in this book includes:

★ a list of skills that highlights the math focus of each lesson.

★ a complete list of materials needed for each lesson.

★ setup instructions, easy how-to's, and helpful tips to ensure that activities go smoothly.

★ ideas, strategies, and lessons for using the nursery rhyme to teach key math concepts and skills.

★ fun and interactive activities, games, and manipulatives that give children practice with specific concepts and skills. Most include ready-to-copy patterns.

★ extension activities and learning center suggestions that provide additional opportunities to reinforce concepts and skills.

★ literature connections to extend learning.

Connections With the NCTM Standards

The National Council of Teachers of Mathematics (NCTM) has outlined ten content and process standards that have become the basis for change in the way mathematics is taught and in how children in grades K–2 are learning mathematics. Use the chart below to see at a glance how each lesson in this book correlates with the standards.

Nursery Rhyme	Number and Operations	Patterns and Algebra	Geometry and Spatial Sense	Measurement	Data Analysis and Probability	Problem Solving	Reasoning and Proof	Communication	Connections	Representation
One, Two, Buckle My Shoe	✻							✻	✻	✻
Three Little Kittens	✻	✻				✻	✻	✻	✻	✻
Old Mother Hubbard	✻	✻					✻	✻	✻	✻
The Queen of Hearts	✻	✻	✻				✻	✻	✻	✻
Little Bo-Peep	✻			✻			✻	✻	✻	✻
Mistress Mary	✻	✻			✻	✻	✻	✻	✻	✻
Wee Willie Winkie	✻				✻				✻	✻
Simple Simon	✻	✻	✻				✻	✻	✻	✻
To Banbury Cross	✻					✻	✻	✻	✻	✻
Mrs. Hen	✻	✻				✻	✻	✻	✻	✻

One, Two, Buckle My Shoe

One, two,
Buckle my shoe.
Three, four,
Shut the door.
Five, six,
Pick up sticks.
Seven, eight,
Lay them straight.
Nine, ten,
A big fat hen.

Mother Goose Math   Scholastic Professional Books

One, Two, Buckle My Shoe

Getting Ready

1 Photocopy the rhyme on page 6 for each child, and write the rhyme on chart paper.

2 Make copies of the shoe pattern pages for each child.

Reading the Rhyme

1 Read aloud the rhyme, tracking the print as you read. Then, as you reread it, invite children to pantomine the actions described in the rhyme.

2 Read the rhyme again, pointing to the number words, and invite children to read them with you. Then try the following activities to help children gain familiarity with the numbers 1 to 10.

3 Use a self-sticking note to mask one of the numbers mentioned in the rhyme, and challenge children to tell the number that is missing.

4 Ask a volunteer to come up and circle the word *one*. Then ask children if they can think of another way to write *one* ("1" or a mark or picture to indicate a single object). Write their ideas on self-sticking notes and place them over the word *one* in the rhyme. Continue in this manner for the remaining number words.

5 Ask children questions about the numbers in the rhyme, such as "What number comes right after two? What number comes right before seven? What number comes between eight and ten?"

❖ Buckle-Your-Shoe Book ❖

1 Hand out the two shoe pattern pages to each child. Tell children to cut out the strap and set it aside. Then have them cut out the shoe patterns.

SKILLS

recognizing, writing, and understanding numbers

counting to 10

MATERIALS

★ chart paper
★ markers
★ self-sticking notes

For each child:

★ shoe patterns, pages 9–10
★ scissors
★ crayons or markers
★ brass fastener

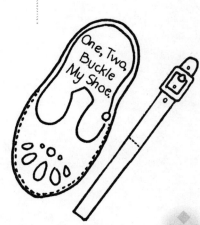

2 Invite children to read the text on each shoe and then put the pages in order with the cover on top. Check each child's book, and have children staple their book along the left side. Then have them punch a hole through all pages of the book at once, using the circle on the cover as a guide.

3 Provide crayons or markers and tell children to trace the numerals 1 and 2 on the first page of their book. Then ask children to write the numeral for each of the remaining number words in their book.

4 To "buckle" their shoe book, have children first fold their strap in half along the dotted line. Then have them punch a hole through the folded strap at the circle on the buckle end. Holding the buckle side of the strap faceup, children slip the spine of their book inside the folded part of the strap, aligning the punched holes on the strap with the hole in the book. Children can then poke a brass fastener through the holes in the strap and the book pages and spread open the prongs on the back of their book.

5 To practice reading their books, have children unbuckle their shoes and read aloud the rhyme to a partner. Then invite children to take their shoe books home to share with their family.

Mother Goose Learning Center

One, Two, Lace Up the Shoe! Give children more practice with numbers. Enlarge and copy a shoe pattern on page 9, masking the text, and then glue it to cardboard. Punch ten holes down each side of the shoe. Label the holes on the left with a numeral between 1 and 10, out of order. On the right side, label the corresponding number sets (and/or number words), also out of order. Cut five shoelaces in half, then thread each piece through a hole on the left side of the shoe and secure from the back with a knot. Place the shoe in a center and invite children to match each numeral to its number set by threading each shoelace through the hole beside its corresponding number set.

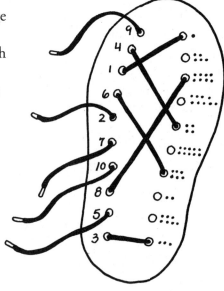

Buckle-Your-Shoe Book

shoe patterns

One, Two, Buckle My Shoe

1 2

One, two,

Buckle my shoe.

②

Three, four,

Shut the door.

③

Mother Goose Math
Scholastic Professional Books

9

Buckle-Your-Shoe Book

strap pattern

shoe patterns

Five, six,

Pick up sticks.

④

Seven, eight,

Lay them straight.

⑤

Nine, ten,

A big fat hen.

⑥

Mother Goose Math
Scholastic Professional Books

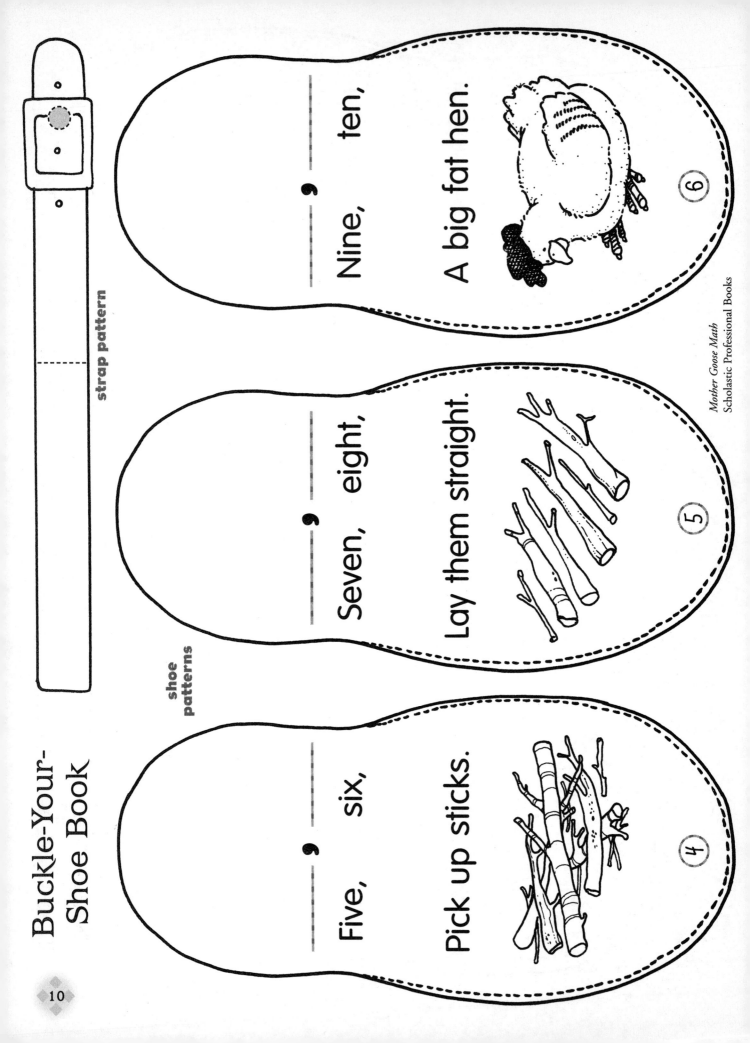

Three Little Kittens

Three little kittens lost their mittens,
And they began to cry,
"Oh, mother dear,
We sadly fear
That we have lost our mittens!"

"You lost your mittens?
You naughty kittens!
Then you shall have no pie."

"Mee-ow, mee-ow, mee-ow.
We shall have no pie."

The three little kittens found their mittens,
And they began to cry,
"Oh, mother dear,
See here, see here,
We have found our mittens!"

"You found your mittens?
You good little kittens.
Then you shall have some pie."

"Purr-r, purr-r, purr-r,
We shall have some pie!"

Three Little Kittens

SKILLS

one-to-one correspondence

skip-counting

sorting by attributes

patterning

MATERIALS

★ chart paper
★ marker
★ pairs of mittens (one pair for each child, if possible)

For each child:

★ kitten and mitten patterns, page 15
★ crayons, colored pencils, or markers
★ large sheet of construction paper
★ scissors
★ glue stick

Getting Ready

1 Photocopy the rhyme on page 11 for each child, and write the rhyme on chart paper.

2 Ahead of time, ask each child to bring in one or more pairs of mittens to use in Reading the Rhyme, below. (If it's not possible to use real mittens, make multiple copies of the kitten and mitten patterns on page 15.)

Reading the Rhyme

1 Read the rhyme once. Then reread it, inviting children to chime in when the kittens meow and purr.

2 Ask for three volunteers to be the kittens and one to be their mother. Give each kitten a pair of mittens. Then invite children to act out the rhyme as you read it again.

3 To help reinforce the concept of one-to-one correspondence, ask, "How many mittens does each kitten have?" (*two, one for each paw*) Then ask "How many pairs are there?" (*three*) "How many mittens are there in all?" (*6*)

4 Tell the kittens to form a line, and to hold up their mittened paws as you model skip-counting by twos. Then encourage children to skip-count with you.

5 Now invite two more children to be kittens and give them mittens to put on. Read the rhyme again, changing the number of kittens to five. Then skip-count, inviting children to predict what number will come next as each new kitten holds up his or her mittened paws.

6 Now have the entire class sit in a circle and become kittens wearing mittens. As you walk around the circle, skip-count the mittens, inviting children to join in. Then ask children why we sometimes count by twos instead of ones. (*It's an easier and faster way to count and keep track of bigger numbers.*)

Mittens for Kittens ❖

1 Give each child three copies of the kitten and mitten pattern page, scissors, coloring supplies, a sheet of construction paper, and a glue stick. Tell children to cut out the kittens and to color each pair of mittens using a different color of crayon.

2 Ask children if they have enough mittens for their kittens' front paws. To check, have children match up each pair of mittens to the kittens' paws. Then have children glue the kittens in their mittens onto the construction paper.

3 Ask a volunteer to stand up and hold up his or her work. As a class, skip-count by 2s the mittens on the child's paper. Then ask another child to stand and repeat the process, beginning with the first student again. Continue in this manner until the entire class is standing and you have counted all the mittens by twos. Afterward, create a "Skip-Counting Kitten Mittens" bulletin board using students' papers. Mount them side by side, low enough for students to reach, and then invite children, in turn, to write the corresponding numbers (2, 4, 6, and so on) above each of their kittens on their papers.

More Math Fun!

Mitten Match-Up Warm up children's classification skills with this sorting activity. Gather together an assortment of mittens and/or gloves in different colors and patterns (or enlarge the mitten patterns on page 15). Give each child a pair to put on. Ask children to describe attributes of the class's mittens (red, orange, striped, polka-dotted, and so on). Make a list of children's responses. Then pick an attribute (for example, polka dots/no polka dots) to use to sort the mittens into two groups—but keep it a secret from your class. Then direct children, in turn, to place their mittens in the appropriate group. After five or six pairs have been sorted, ask the remaining children to pick the group in which they think their mittens belong. If children choose incorrectly, direct them to put their mittens in the correct pile. Then, after sorting all the mittens, ask children to guess the attribute you used, guiding them with clues if they need help. Then repeat the activity using another attribute.

Activity adapted from "Why Do Mittens Work?" by Lynne Kepler, *Instructor Magazine*, January/February 1996.

Mother Goose Book Nook

Here are two great books for extending the concept of one-to-one correspondence:

One of Each by Mary Ann Hoberman (Little, Brown, 1997). Oliver Tolliver is content living in his own little house. After all, he has one of everything he needs—one table, one chair, one closet, one stair. But when Peggoty Small comes to visit, Oliver discovers that his "one-of-each house [is] not suited for two."

Hannah and the Seven Dresses by Marthe Jocelyn (Penguin Putnam, 1999). Young Hannah loves to wear dresses and her mother loves to sew. That means Hannah has seven beautiful dresses, one to wear every day of the week! But on her birthday, Hannah faces a dress dilemma: Which one should she wear?

Mother Goose Learning Center

Mitten Patterns

Copy additional verses of the "Three Little Kittens" rhyme on chart paper (see below), and read the rhyme with children. Then, at a center, tie a length of string between two chairs. On one chair, place a basket filled with multiple enlarged copies of the mitten patterns on page 15 (or use real pairs of mittens in different patterns and colors). On the other chair, provide a basket of spring-type clothespins and paper and crayons. Invite children to come to the center, color the mittens as desired, and then "hang them up to dry" by clipping them to the clothesline to create different patterns. Encourage children to draw pictures of the patterns they made.

The three little kittens
put on their mittens,
And soon ate up the pie.
"Oh, mother dear,
We sadly fear
That we have soiled our mittens."

"Soiled your mittens?
You naughty kittens!"

Then they began to sigh,
"Mee-ow, mee-ow, mee-ow."
Then they began to sigh.

The three little kittens
Washed their mittens,
And hung them up to dry.
"Oh, mother dear,
Do you not hear,
That we have washed our mittens?"

"Washed your mittens!
Oh, you good little kittens.
Now you can play outside."

Mittens
for Kittens

kitten pattern

mitten patterns

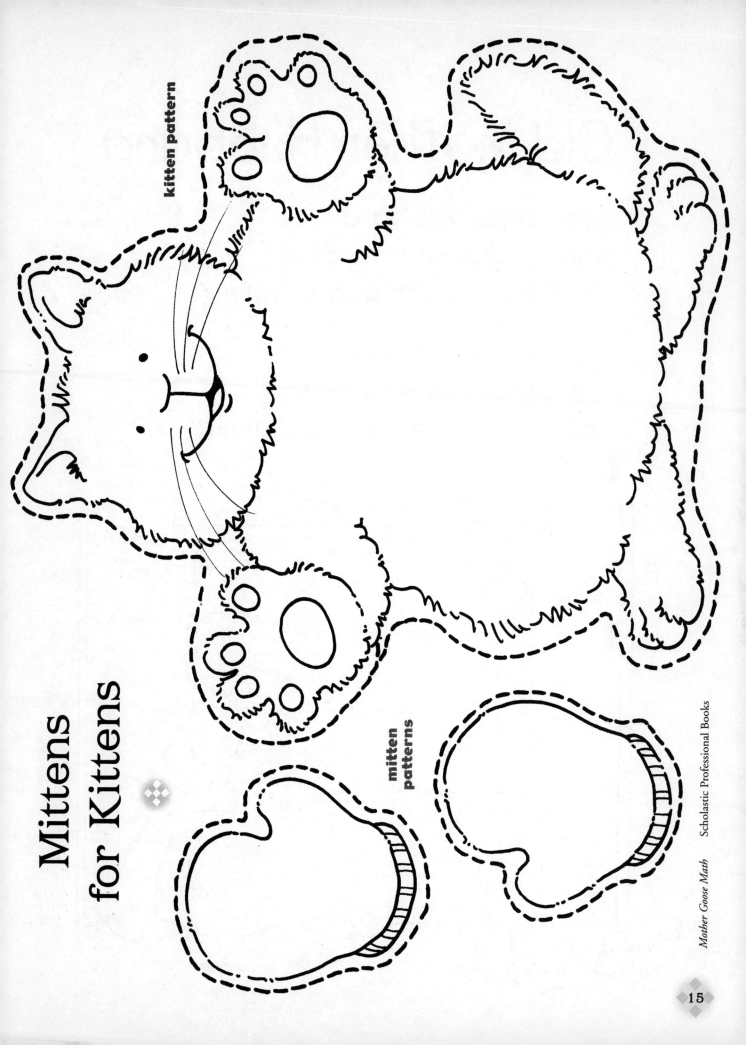

Old Mother Hubbard

Old Mother Hubbard
Went to the cupboard
To give her poor dog a bone.

But when she got there,
The cupboard was bare,
And so the poor dog had none.

Mother Goose Math   Scholastic Professional Books

Old Mother Hubbard

Getting Ready

1 Photocopy the rhyme on page 16 for each child, and write the rhyme on chart paper.

2 Make a cupboard by taping the lid to the shoe box along one long side. To make a hinged door, slit the lid at the two corners on the side that is taped to the box. Decorate to resemble a cupboard.

3 Place the dog bones (or bone patterns) in the paper bag. Make a copy of the pattern pages for each student pair.

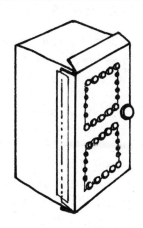

Reading the Rhyme

1 Read aloud the rhyme and then invite children to join in as you reread it. Let a volunteer hold the toy dog, open the shoe box cupboard, and tell the class what he or she finds inside. (*nothing*) Ask children to find the word in the rhyme that means "nothing." (*none*)

2 Ask: "Do you know another word that means the same thing as *none*? (*zero*) Write the word on the chart paper. Then ask: "What is another way to show zero?" Let a volunteer come up to the chart and draw a zero, or draw the symbol yourself.

3 Tell children to close their eyes. Then put two dog bones inside the cupboard. Repeat steps 1 to 3. Do this a few more times with different quantities.

Old Mother Hubbard Counting Cupboard

1 Give each pair of children a copy of the cupboard, dog and bowl, and bone patterns to color and cut out. Also provide a 6-inch square of construction paper and a small bag (for storing the bones between uses).

SKILLS

mixed practice (counting, skip-counting, addition and subtraction, fact families, making sets)

MATERIALS

★ chart paper
★ marker
★ shoe box with lid
★ tape
★ scissors
★ mini dog bones (or use the bone patterns on page 21)
★ paper lunch bag
★ stuffed toy dog (optional)

For each student pair:

★ cupboard, dog and bowl, and bone patterns, pages 20–21
★ scissors
★ crayons or markers
★ 6-inch construction paper square
★ ruler
★ tape
★ small paper bag

2 Show children how to cut open the doors to the cupboard along the dotted lines and fold them back. (An easy way to cut the doors is to fold the paper at a right angle to the dotted lines. Then snip along the lines from the crease of the fold inward.) Next, have children place the cupboard facedown and tape the construction paper to the back.

3 For shelves, students can use a marker and ruler to draw three horizontal lines, evenly spaced on the construction paper.

4 Show children how to fold up their dog so that it sits in front of its bowl. Then have them spread out the dog bones. (Children can store their bones in a small paper bag between uses.)

5 Use the manipulatives with children to help reinforce and practice a variety of skills and concepts. For example:

★ **Counting** Give each child a dog and bowl. Children begin by putting a given number of bones in the cupboard. Then they take turns tossing a 1 to 6 number cube and placing the corresponding number of bones in their dog's bowl. After three or four turns, children count up the bones to see whose dog has the most.

★ **Skip-Counting** On each side of the cupboard, have children put two (or three) bones on each shelf. Then have them count by 2s (or 3s).

★ **Addition and Subtraction** Have children pose simple story problems for each other to solve. For example:

● *Two Addends* "Mother Hubbard put two bones on the left side of the cupboard and three bones on the right side. How many bones are there in all?"

● *Three Addends* "Mother Hubbard put one bone on the left side of the cupboard, two bones on the right side, and four bones in the bowl. How many bones are there in all?"

● *Addition Fact Families* Have children work with a given number of bones—for example, ten. Ask them to use the bones to show different ways to make ten. Tell children to keep track of the ways they come up with by recording them on paper.

● *Subtraction* "There are seven bones in the cupboard. Mother Hubbard's dog is hungry. So she puts five bones in its bowl. How many bones are left in the cupboard?"

● *Missing Addends* Have children work with a given number of bones. Let them take turns placing some of the bones in the cupboard (without letting their partners see), and the rest in the bowl. The partners then try to figure out how many bones are in the cupboard.

★ **Making Sets** Give partners two sets of bones, each consisting of a different even number. Tell them to divide one set evenly between the shelves on one side of the cupboard. Have them count and record the amount on each shelf. Then they repeat this process with the second set of bones on the other side of the cupboard. Have them compare and discuss their results.

6 After working with the manipulatives, place them in a learning center for children to work with independently, in pairs, or in small groups.

More Math Fun!

Doggy Lineup This activity will help children sharpen listening skills and practice ordering numbers. Make ten copies of the dog and bowl pattern for each child and one set for yourself. (To save paper, reduce the pattern to fit ten on one page.) Have children cut apart the dogs and bowls. Then, using ten different-colored crayons (orange, dark blue, yellow, green, red, brown, purple, light blue, black, and pink), direct children to color each of their dogs a different color, while you do the same. Children then place the bowls in a row. Keeping them hidden from children's view, place your dogs in a row, in any order. Tell children to match up the dogs with their bowls by following directions you call out. For example, "The purple dog is third. The light blue dog is last. The blue dog goes before the purple dog."

❖ Mother Goose Learning Center ❖

Boning Up on Numbers To help reinforce the numbers you want children to learn, make extra copies of the dog and bowl and bone patterns on page 21. Cut apart the dogs and bowls. Label each dog with a numeral and the side of the bowl with the corresponding number word. Laminate or paste to cardboard for durability. Place the bones in a paper bag labeled "Dog Bones." Invite children to visit the center, match the dogs to their bowls, and place the corresponding number of bones in the bowl.

Mother Goose Book Nook

12 Ways to Get to 11 by Eve Merriam (Simon & Schuster, 1993). What comes out of the magician's hat? "Four banners, five rabbits, a pitcher of water, and a bouquet of flowers." In this delightful book, young readers learn that there are lots of unusual and funny ways to get to 11. Bright and bold collage illustrations depict different combinations of objects that each total 11.

What is Nana Quimby to do? One cat, then five cats, then ten cats, and then more and more cats are getting stuck in her tree! Kids will love to skip-count felines by fives in the whimsical story **Cat up a Tree**, by John Hassett (Houghton Mifflin, 1998).

Old Mother Hubbard Counting Cupboard

Mother Goose Math   Scholastic Professional Books

cupboard pattern

bone patterns

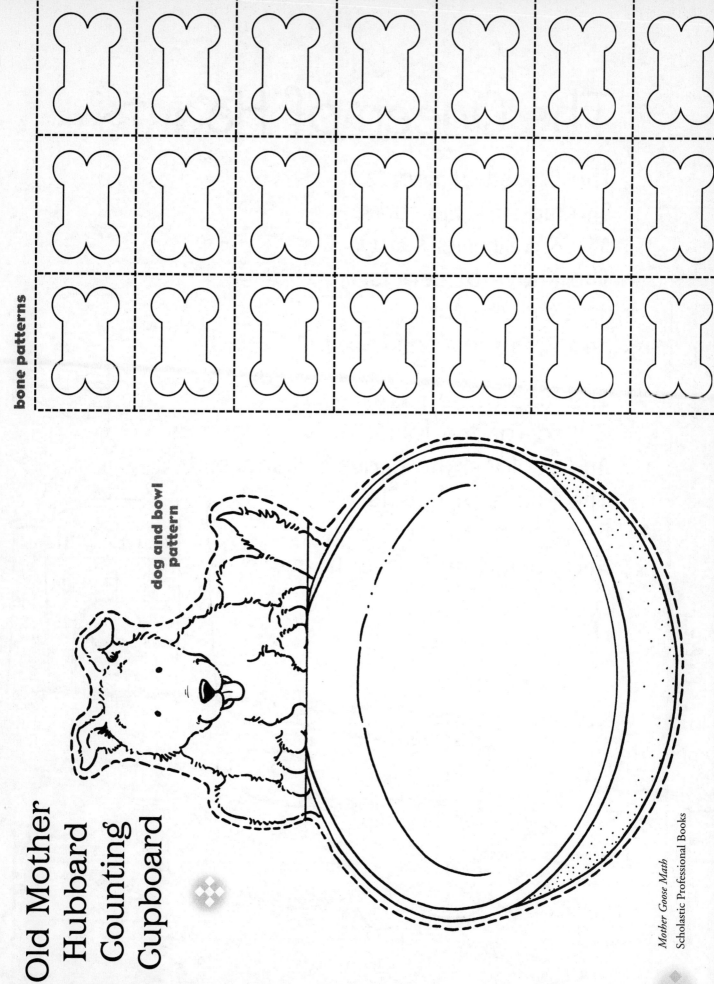

Old Mother Hubbard Counting Cupboard

dog and bowl pattern

The Queen of Hearts

The Queen of Hearts,
She made some tarts,
All on a summer's day;
The Knave of Hearts,
He stole the tarts,
And with them ran away.

The King of Hearts
Called for the tarts,
And scolded the Knave full score.
The Knave of Hearts
Brought back the tarts,
And vowed he'd steal no more.

Mother Goose Math
Scholastic Professional Books

The Queen of Hearts

Getting Ready

1 Make a copy of the rhyme on page 22 for each child, and write the rhyme on chart paper.

2 Make a copy of the ten tarts on page 26 for each child. Make an extra copy and cut out the tarts, coloring them if you like. Then place them on a tray or plate. (Or use jam-filled cookies instead.)

Reading the Rhyme

1 Read aloud the nursery rhyme. Then discuss words and phrases that may be unfamiliar to children, such as *tart* (a pastry similar to a small pie, filled with jam or fruit), *knave* (a boy who is a servant; someone who is tricky or dishonest), *full score* (20 times), and *vowed* (promised). Then show children the Queen, King, and Jack playing cards. Explain that this rhyme brings these playing card characters to life and that *jack* is another word for knave.

2 Discuss what happens in the rhyme. Ask children what they think of the Knave's behavior. Why did the Knave return the tarts? Do they think he learned a lesson?

3 Using self-sticking notes, replace words in the rhyme with different numbers to create subtraction story problems for children to solve. For example:

> The Queen of Hearts,
> She made 5 tarts,
> All on a summer's day;
> The Knave of Hearts,
> He stole 3 tarts,
> And with them ran away.

4 Put the tray of "tarts" on a table and read the revised version of the rhyme. Invite pairs of children to act out the math problem. Then ask: "How many tarts were left?" (*2*) On the chalkboard, write a subtraction sentence to represent the math word problem symbolically. (*5 – 3 = 2*)

MATERIALS

- ★ chart paper
- ★ marker
- ★ self-sticking notes
- ★ tart patterns, page 26 (or jam-filled cookies)
- ★ crayons, colored pencils, or markers
- ★ tray or large plate
- ★ Queen, King, and Jack playing cards

For each child:

- ★ scissors
- ★ crayons, colored pencils, or markers
- ★ paper plate
- ★ glue sticks

5 Challenge children further by substituting numerals in the second verse of the rhyme as well. For example:

> The King of Hearts
> called for the tarts,
> and scolded the Knave full score.
> The Knave of Hearts
> brought back 2 tarts,
> and vowed he'd steal no more.

6 Ask children how many tarts the Knave did not bring back. (*1*) Invite them to speculate about what happened to the last tart! Then, on the chalkboard, write the addition sentence to represent the addition problem. (*2 + 2 = 4*)

7 Repeat this process, letting other groups of children act out different math problems and, afterward, writing the equations on the chalkboard. (To work with higher numbers, make additional copies of the tart patterns.)

✦ Keep Track of the Tarts! ✦

1 Make an extra copy of the rhyme for each child, masking out the words *some* in line 2 and *the* in lines 5 and 10. Give each child a copy of the ten tarts to color and cut out. Also give each child a paper plate.

2 Invite children to work with partners, first thinking of numbers to write in the blank spaces on their poetry page and then discussing whether each of their number choices makes sense in the rhyme (for example, the Knave couldn't take 7 tarts if the Queen had only baked 2). Then have children write in the numbers and then read aloud each of their revised rhymes as they place and remove tart patterns to correspond with the actions in the rhyme.

More Math Fun!

Candy-Heart Tart Flash Cards Children will love this sweet way to practice fact families! Glue candy conversation hearts to index cards (or draw hearts instead) to illustrate different fact families (for example, 2 + 4, 3 + 3, and 1 + 5 are fact families for the number 6). Distribute a card to each child. Challenge children to find other classmates who have cards from the same fact family. Later, put the cards in a learning center and invite students to visit and sort the cards into fact family groups.

❖ Missing Shape Match-Up Game ❖

1 Provide a copy of the game board plate on page 27 to each student pair.

2 Discuss with children the names of each shape on their plate. Talk about one shape at a time. Starting with the circle, for example, ask questions such as "Can you find this shape in our classroom? Where else have you seen this shape? How would you describe this shape?"

3 Give each child a copy of the ten tarts on page 26. Also give each student pair two different-colored crayons. Have children each color their tarts with one color and cut them out.

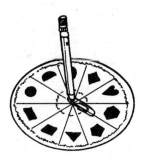

4 Give each pair a copy of the spinner on page 26, a paper clip, and a pencil. Model how to use the spinner.

5 Introduce the game by telling children that the Queen of Hearts is upset because her fresh-baked tarts are missing. Their job is to help her find the tarts and return them to their correct place on the plate.

6 To play, children take turns spinning, selecting the tart that has the shape pictured, naming it if they can, and placing it on a matching shape on the plate.

7 If a player spins a shape that has already been filled, the player misses a turn. The winner is the player who has the most tarts on the plate when all the shapes have been covered.

More Math Fun!

Shape Tarts Bring in an assortment of plain cookies and crackers in different shapes (circles, ovals, diamonds, rectangles, squares). At snacktime, invite children to choose a cookie for their tart. Then provide jam and plastic spoons for them to spread a spoonful of jam on their cookie or cracker. Top off the shape tarts with a dollop of whipped cream. Invite each child to describe the shape of his or her tart and then munch away! (Check for food allergies before doing this activity, and provide substitute snacks if needed.)

SKILLS

identifying attributes of shapes

MATERIALS

For each student pair:
★ game board, spinner, and tart patterns, pages 26–27
★ paper clip
★ pencil
★ scissors
★ crayons (two different colors)

Mother Goose Book Nook

Round is a Mooncake: A Book of Shapes by Roseanne Thong (Chronicle Books, 2002). Children will have fun identifying different shapes as represented by round rice bowls, square dim sum, and other items in Chinese culture.

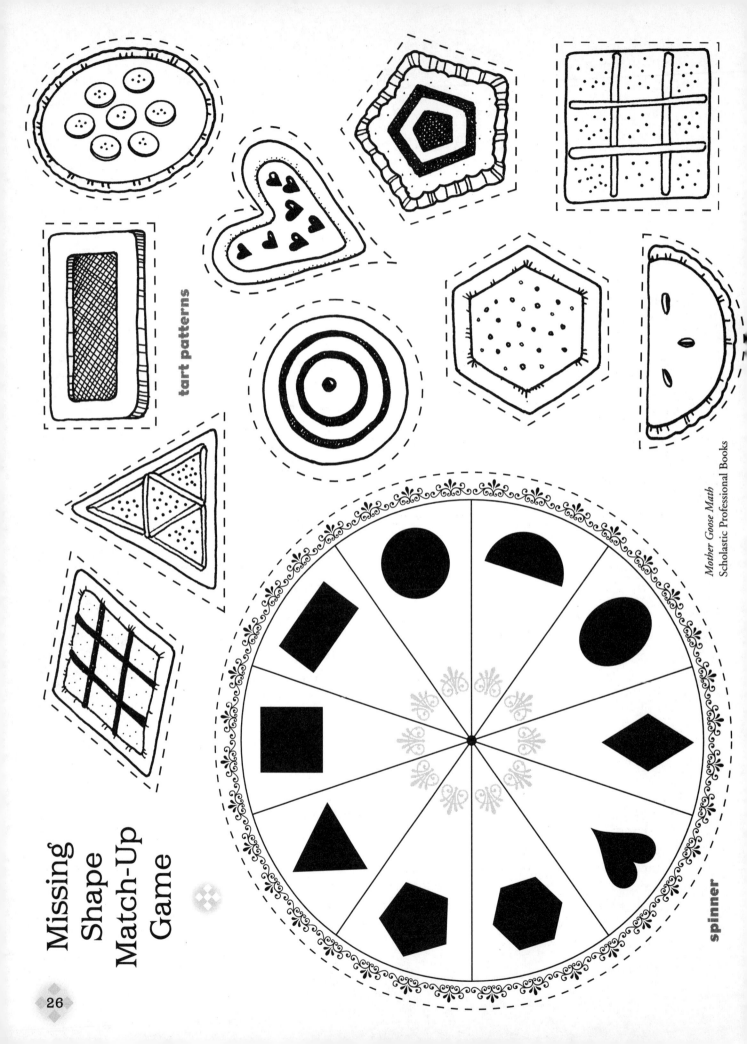

tart patterns

Missing Shape Match-Up Game

spinner

26

Missing Shape Match-Up Game

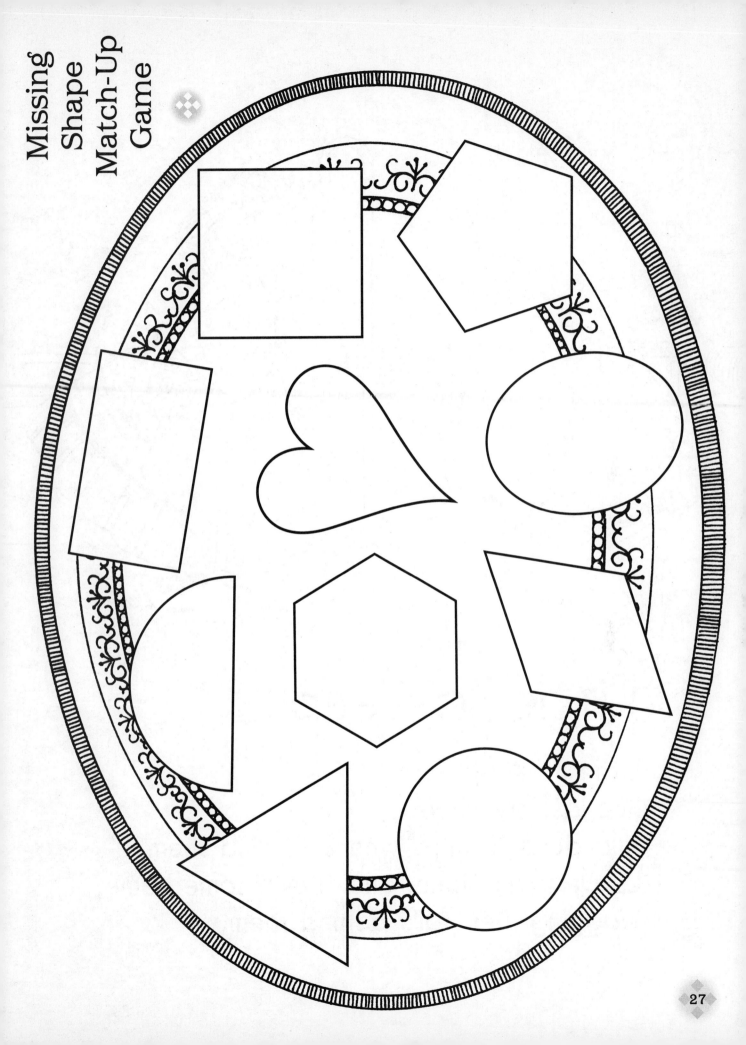

Little Bo-Peep

Little Bo-Peep
Has lost her sheep,
And doesn't know where to find them.
Leave them alone, and they'll come home,
Wagging their tails behind them.

Mother Goose Math

Scholastic Professional Books

Little Bo-Peep

Getting Ready

1 Photocopy the rhyme on page 28 for each child, and write the rhyme on chart paper.

2 On another sheet of chart paper, draw a grid that has four rows and four columns. Label the rows from bottom to top, 1 to 4. Then label the columns from left to right, A to D.

3 Make a copy of the sheep pattern, enlarging it to fit inside one of the squares on the chart paper grid. Then place the sheep in square (D, 3) using removable adhesive or tape.

4 Make copies of page 31 for each child. Laminate the game board grids to make them reusable.

Reading the Rhyme

1 Read aloud the rhyme. Then ask children to reread it with you. Ask them where they think Bo-Peep has lost her sheep. How might she find them?

2 Show children the chart paper grid. Point out the letters and numbers and explain that these can be used to name each square on the grid. Point out (A, 1) and (A, 2) as examples.

3 Ask the class to pretend that this is a map that shows where Bo-Peep has lost one of her sheep. Can they help Bo-Peep find her lost sheep? Ask children to name the square where the sheep is located.

4 Point to column D and then run your finger up the column, counting aloud as you move up the rows from (D, 1) to (D, 3).

5 Change the sheep's location on the grid and repeat the activity several times.

SKILL

coordinate geometry

MATERIALS

★ chart paper
★ marker
★ removable adhesive or tape

For each child:

★ game board and sheep patterns, page 31
★ scissors
★ crayons or markers

Find Bo-Peep's Sheep!

Tip

Give each child an extra copy of the game board. Children can use a crayon to record correct and incorrect guesses on the extra grid, using a different color for each.

1 Give each child a copy of page 31, scissors, and coloring supplies. Have children color the game board and sheep, as desired, and then cut them out.

2 Divide the class into pairs. Have children sit back-to-back so they can't see each other's game boards. Children then "hide" each of their three sheep in a different square on their game board grid.

3 Explain to children that their job is to find Bo-Peep's sheep on their partner's board. To begin, Player 1 names a grid square—for example, (B, 3). If Player 1 correctly names a square with a sheep, Player 2 says, "Baaaaa!" Player 1 then takes another turn. If Player 1 is incorrect, then Player 2 takes a turn.

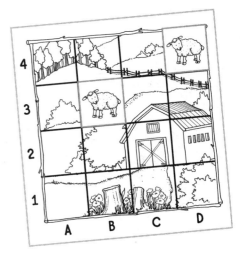

4 Play continues in this manner until all of Bo-Peep's sheep have been found.

5 After playing the game, ask children to describe strategies they used.

Mother Goose Learning Center

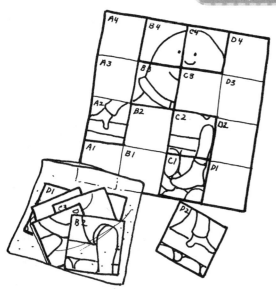

Help Humpty Dumpty Puzzle Use the rhyme "Humpty Dumpty" for a different twist on coordinate geometry. On a sheet of paper, create a 16-square grid and label, as shown. Then make a photocopy. On the copy, draw a simple picture of Humpty Dumpty, filling as much of the grid as possible. Then write a letter and number pair inside each square to correspond with the coordinates on the grid. Make multiple copies of both pages. Cut each Humpty Dumpty page into 16 squares and place in a resealable plastic bag. Put the grids and bags at a center. Challenge children to put Humpty Dumpty together again by placing each piece in its correct place on the grid. Students can then glue the pieces in place and color, as desired.

Find Bo-Peep's Sheep!

sheep markers

game board

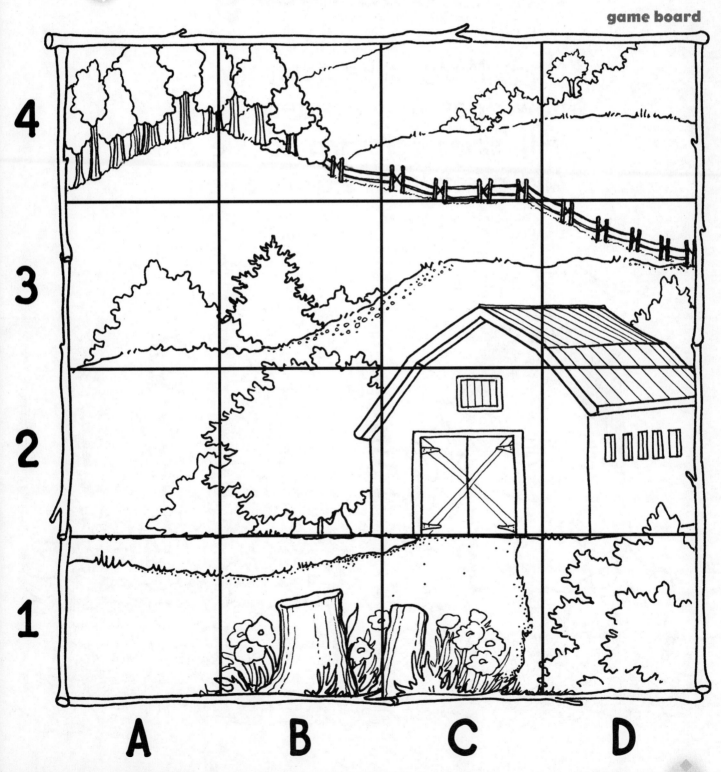

4

3

2

1

A   B   C   D

Mistress Mary

Mary, Mary, quite contrary,
How does your garden grow?
With silver bells and cockle shells,
And pretty maids all in a row.

Mother Goose Math   Scholastic Professional Books

Mistress Mary

Getting Ready

1 Make a copy of the rhyme on page 32 for each child, and write the rhyme on chart paper.

2 Photocopy page 35 for each child.

Reading the Rhyme

1 Read aloud the rhyme with children. Discuss words that may be unfamiliar to them, such as *contrary* and *cockle shells*. If possible, have some cockle-shaped seashells on hand for children to examine. Then have children look at the pictures on their poetry page and ask, "Have you ever seen flowers that look like the ones in this garden? Why do you think they are called cockle shells and silver bells?"

2 Invite children to share experiences they may have had growing plants. Then tell them that they are each going to "plant" a pretend flower for Mistress Mary and measure its growth.

❖ Grow-and-Measure Garden ❖

1 Give each child a copy of the pattern page. Have children glue the page to lightweight cardboard for added durability. Then direct them to cut out the flowerpot, the flower, and the two sections of the ruler. Guide children in taping the parts of the ruler together.

2 Have children cut a slit along the dotted line at the top of the flowerpot. Then have them slide the flower into the pot so that just the flower head sticks out.

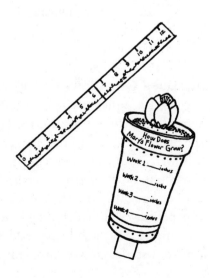

SKILLS

measuring length

MATERIALS

★ chart paper
★ marker
★ seashells (optional)

For each child:

★ flowerpot, flower, and ruler patterns, page 35
★ lightweight cardboard
★ glue stick
★ scissors
★ tape
★ crayons or markers

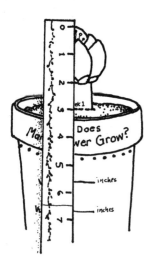

3 Ask children to find out how much Mary's flower grew the first week. To make their flower "grow," have children pull the stem up to the WEEK 1 line. Then guide them in using their ruler to measure and record the flower's height. (*three inches*) Check that children line up the "0" on the ruler with the top of the flower's head, hold the ruler straight, and find where the WEEK 1 line appears on the ruler. Then have children record the height on the flowerpot chart.

4 Now tell children that two more weeks have passed. Tell them to make the flower "grow" to the WEEK 2 line. How tall is Mary's flower now? (*5 inches*) Ask: "How much did Mary's flower grow since week 1?" (*2 inches*)

5 Have children continue in this manner, measuring and recording the flower's growth for the remaining weeks indicated on the flowerpot.

More Math Fun!

Grow-a-Flower Graph Make four copies of the flower pattern for each child. Tell children to cut the first flower on the WEEK 1 line, the second flower on the WEEK 2 line, and so on. Ask children to put the flowers in order, from shortest to tallest, and then glue them to a sheet of construction paper to make a pictograph of the flower's growth. Ask questions, such as "During which week did Mary's flower grow the most? The least?"

How Does Our Class Grow? Bulletin Board Let children become flowers to track their own growth! At the start of the school year, record the height of each child in your class. Help children measure and cut dark green crepe paper streamers to that length and mount them on a bulletin board. For flowers, each child can paint and decorate a paper plate with construction or tissue paper petals. Then take photos of your students' faces and have students paste these in the center of their flowers. Have students add paper leaves on which they have written their names. At the end of the year, remeasure each child and add a length of light green stem to show how much your students have sprouted!

How Does Mary's Flower Grow?

Week 1 _____ inches

Week 2 _____ inches

Week 3 _____ inches

Week 4 _____ inches

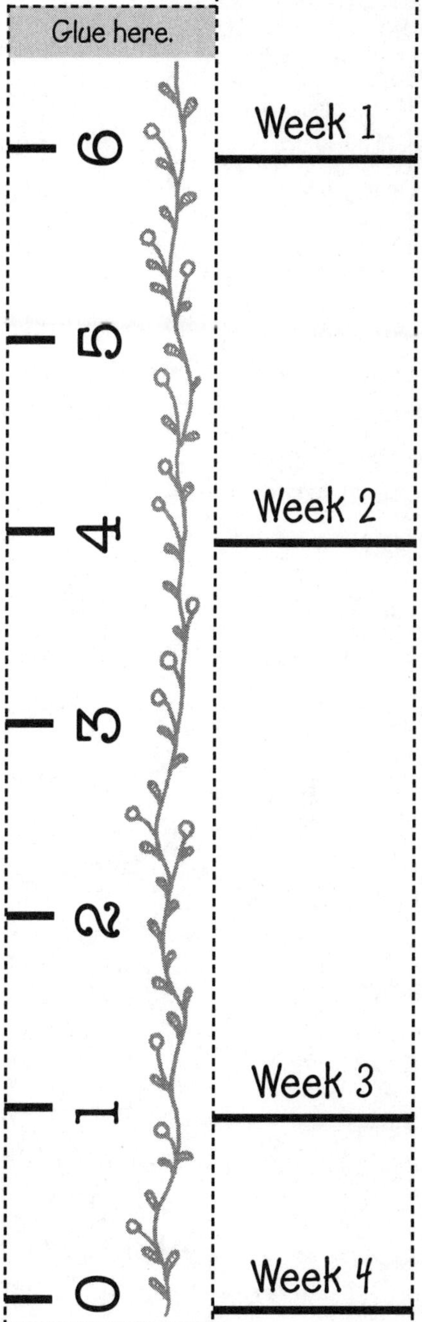

Glue here.

6

5

4

3

2

1

0

Week 1

Week 2

Week 3

Week 4

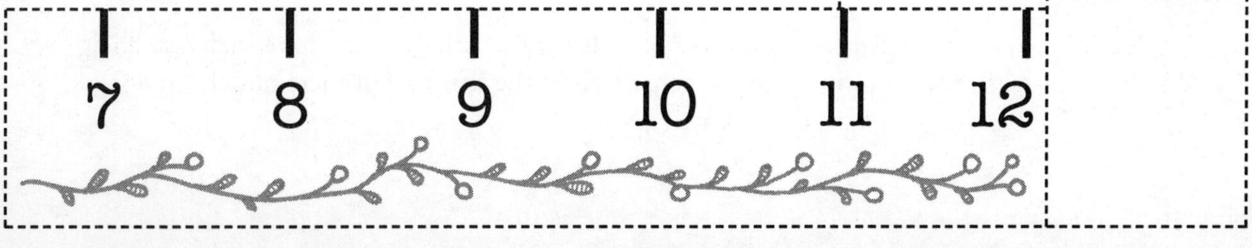

7   8   9   10   11   12

Scholastic Professional Books

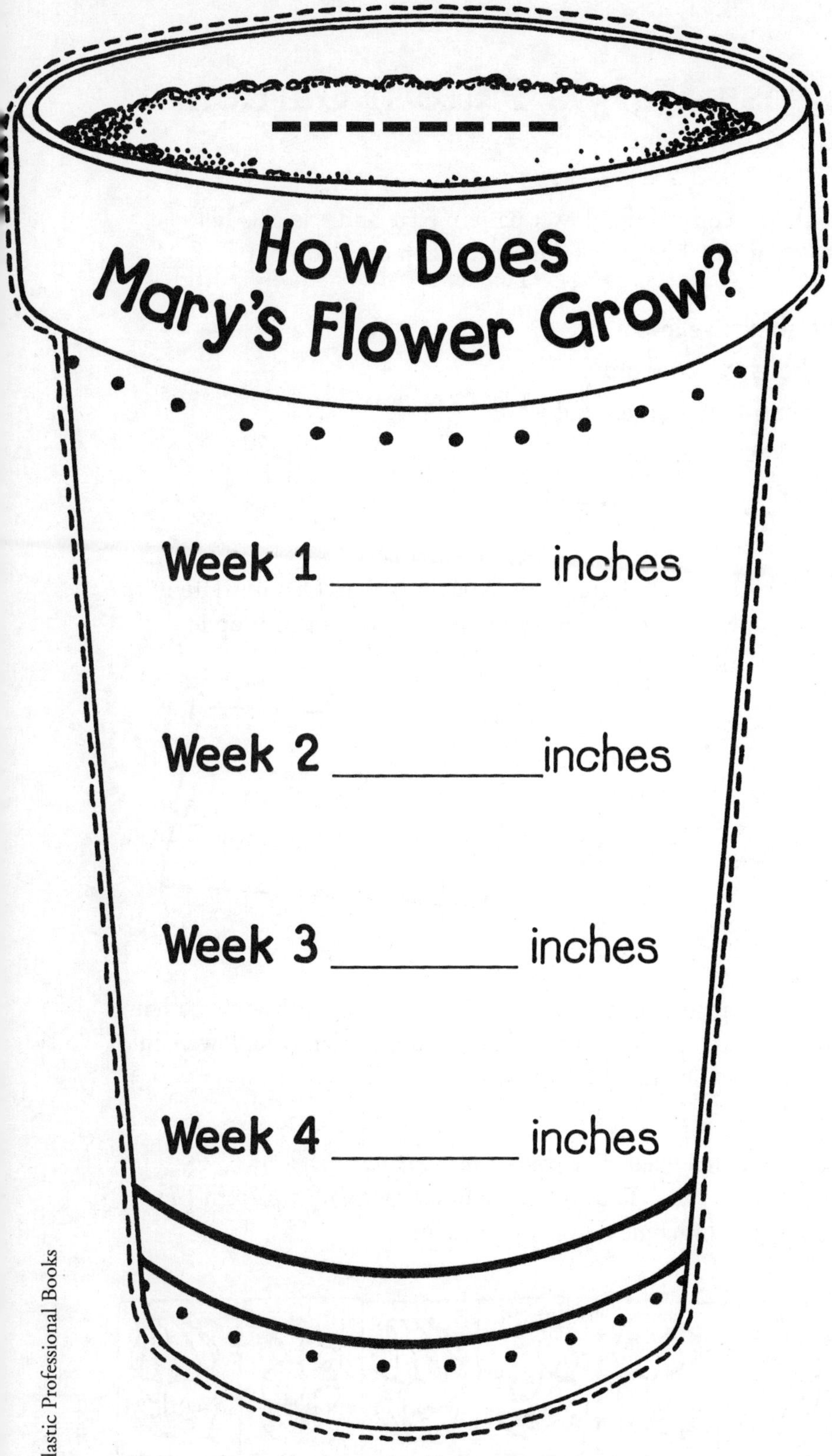

Mistress Mary's Pattern Garden

SKILLS

patterning

MATERIALS

For each child:

★ flower patterns, page 38

★ crayons, colored pencils, or markers

★ scissors

★ sheet of 9- by 12-inch green construction paper

★ glue stick

1 Give each child a copy of the flower pattern page and scissors. Tell children to color the flowers as follows and then cut them out.

cockle shells: yellow
silver bells: silver or gray
peppermint swirls: red and white
snowflakes: leave uncolored
hearts: pink with orange dots

2 Give each child a sheet of green construction paper. Demonstrate how to fold the paper into thirds, horizontally, and then open it up and smooth it out.

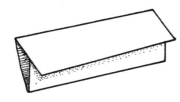

3 Tell children that the folds in the paper are the rows in Mary's garden. Explain that Mary needs their help. She wants to plant the flowers in different patterns—but she can't decide how.

4 Ask students to tell what they think the word *pattern* means. (*something that repeats*) Then ask a volunteer to create a pattern Mary might make using the different flowers. For example:

Let classmates take a look at this child's pattern. Then have them use their flowers to make the same pattern in the first row of their garden.

5 Provide additional examples showing the flowers arranged in other kinds of patterns (by color, kind of flower, number of flowers, and so on).

6 Invite children to experiment with using the flowers to make a different pattern in each row. Encourage them to share their ideas with classmates. When children are satisfied with their arrangements, they can glue the flowers to their paper.

7 Make a bulletin board display with the title "Mary, Mary, How Does Your Pattern Garden Grow?" to showcase children's gardens. Together, discuss the different patterns children made.

Mother Goose Book Nook

Lots and Lots of Zebra Stripes: Patterns in Nature by Stephen R. Swinburne (Boyds Mills Press, 1998). From the stripes on a tiny caterpillar to those in a rainbow stretching across the sky, the beautiful photos in this book show that patterns are everywhere.

More Math Fun!

Pick-a-Pattern Flower Chain Give children more practice in patterning. Make additional copies of the flower pattern page and let children color and cut out the flowers. Then invite them to use a flat surface to create a pattern with the flowers. Give each child an 18-inch length of yarn and glue. Show children how to glue the flowers, in the pattern they created, side by side on the yarn. Then they can knot the ends together to make a colorful flower chain to wear.

Mistress Mary's Pattern Garden

Wee Willie Winkie

Wee Willie Winkie
Runs through the town,
Upstairs and downstairs
In his nightgown,
Rapping at the window,
Crying through the lock,
"Are the children in their beds?
For now it's eight o'clock."

Wee Willie Winkie

SKILL

telling time

MATERIALS

* chart paper
* marker
* self-sticking notes
* paper plate
* brass fastener
* scissors
* lightweight cardboard
* yarn
* nightcap (optional)

For each child:

* town and wheel patterns, pages 43–44
* scissors
* 3 brass fasteners
* lightweight cardboard (optional)
* glue stick (optional)
* crayons or markers

Getting Ready

1 Copy the rhyme on chart paper, and make a photocopy of the rhyme for each child. Set out the display clock near the rhyme. (TIP: If you don't have a display clock, make a simple paper plate clock using a marker, paper hands, and a brass fastener.

2 Make a copy of the town and wheel patterns for each child.

Reading the Rhyme

1 Read aloud the rhyme. When you come to the line "rapping at the window," lightly rap on a hard surface with your fist. Then ask children to tell you what they think the word *rapping* means.

2 Write 8:00 on a self-sticking note next to the words *eight o'clock* in the rhyme. Explain to children that these are both ways of saying the same time. Invite a volunteer to don the nightcap and move the hands on the display clock to show eight o'clock. (TIP: If your school celebrates Pajama Day, this is a great activity to do then!)

3 Ask children to tell their bedtimes. Then read the rhyme again and use self-sticking notes to substitute the time in the rhyme with the times that different children go to bed. For example, "... Are Rosa and Lily in their beds? For now it's seven o'clock." Let volunteers take turns writing the time on self-sticking notes, donning the nightcap, and showing the time on the display clock.

Wee Willie Winkie
Tell-the-Time Wheel

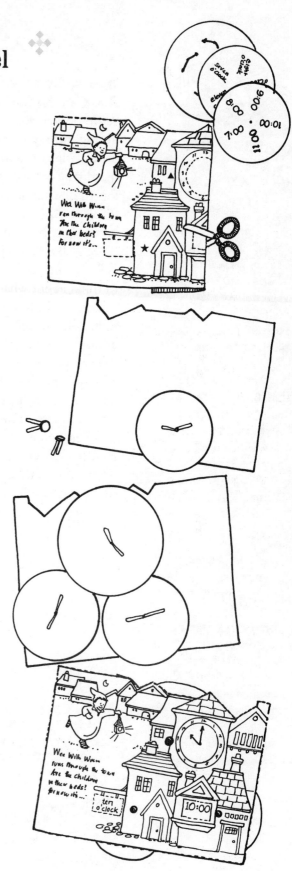

1 Give each child a copy of the pattern pages and scissors. Invite children to color the town scene if they like. (For added durability, let children glue the pages to lightweight cardboard.)

2 Have children cut out the three wheels and the town scene. Then show them how to cut out the three windows in the town, as shown. (An easy way to cut the windows is to lightly fold the paper at a right angle to the dotted lines. Then snip along the lines from the crease of the fold inward.)

3 Give children each three brass fasteners. Show them how to poke a fastener first through the black star marker on the town and then through the black star marker on WHEEL 1, checking to be sure that the words *seven o'clock*, and so on, appear in the window on the front of the town. Children can then bend down the sides of the fastener on the back of the wheel.

4 Have children do the same thing with WHEEL 2 (using the black triangle markers as a guide) and WHEEL 3 (using the black circle markers as a guide).

5 Together, read the abbreviated rhyme on the town scene using eight o'clock as the time. Then demonstrate how to turn WHEEL 1 until *eight o'clock* appears in the top window. Challenge children to turn wheels 2 and 3 so that the digital and analog clocks show the same time.

6 Give children time to turn their wheels and practice making the same time appear in all three windows. Invite volunteers to read the rhyme, substituting the time of their choice, while classmates position their wheels accordingly.

Mother Goose Book Nook

Me Counting Time: From Seconds to Centuries by Joan Sweeney (Crown, 2000). A young girl explains how she tells different amounts of time apart: "A second is like the blink of an eye," a minute is how long it takes her to write a party invitation, an hour is how long it takes to make a cake, and so on.

• • • • • • • • •

What time is it? Poor Mr. Higgins doesn't know. As he races through the rooms of his house, every clock reads a different time! Children will chuckle at the "time" honored classic *Clocks and More Clocks*, by Pat Hutchins (Simon & Schuster, 1994).

Wee Willie at Work Collaborative Book In this fun activity, your students get to decide what Wee Willie calls out during the daytime! On a large sheet of paper, print the abbreviated version of the rhyme on page 43, omitting the fourth line and putting a blank line in its place. Also draw a simple clock face, leaving plenty of room for children to draw. Make multiple copies for each child in your class. Then invite children to think about what Wee Willie might call out first thing in the morning, and then hour by hour during the day. (See examples, right.) Have children write their responses on the blank lines and then, on the clock face, draw clock hands to show the corresponding time. They can also draw a picture showing them engaging in each activity. Guide children in putting the pages in order. Then, after binding to make a book, invite each child to read aloud his or her page.

Wee Willie Winkie
runs through the town.
"Are the children
at their desks?
For now it's 9:00."

Wee Willie Winkie
runs through the town.
"Are the children
having snack?
For now it's 10:00."

Wee Willie Winkie
runs through the town.
"Are the children
having lunch?
For now it's 12:00."

Wee Willie Winkie
runs through the town.
"Are the children
leaving school?"
For now it's 2:00."

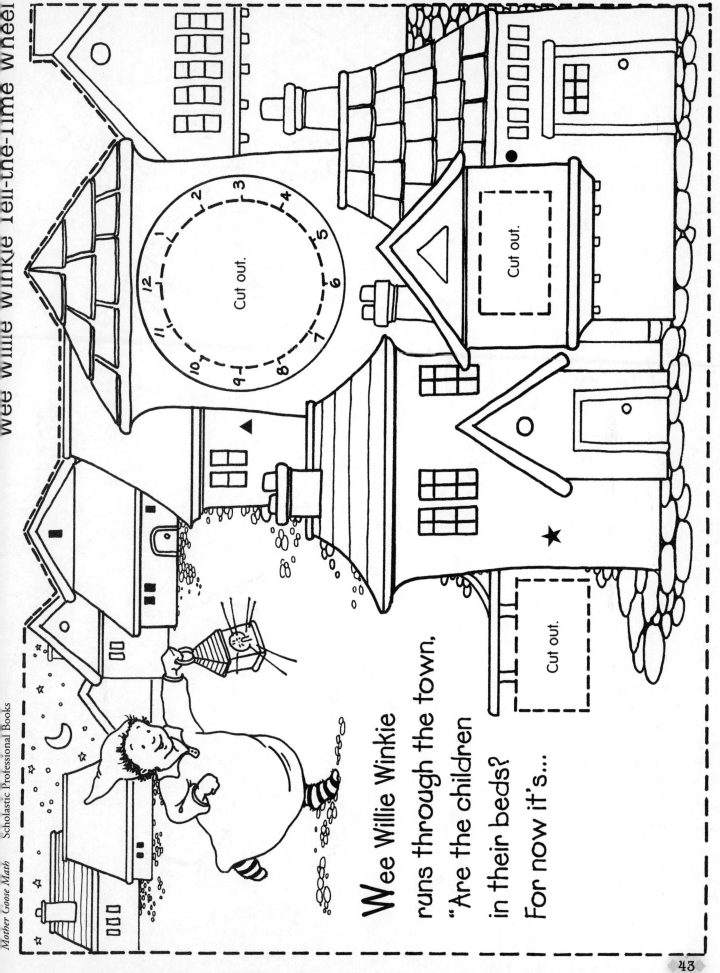

Cut out.

Cut out.

Cut out.

Wee Willie Winkie
runs through the town,
"Are the children
in their beds?
For now it's...

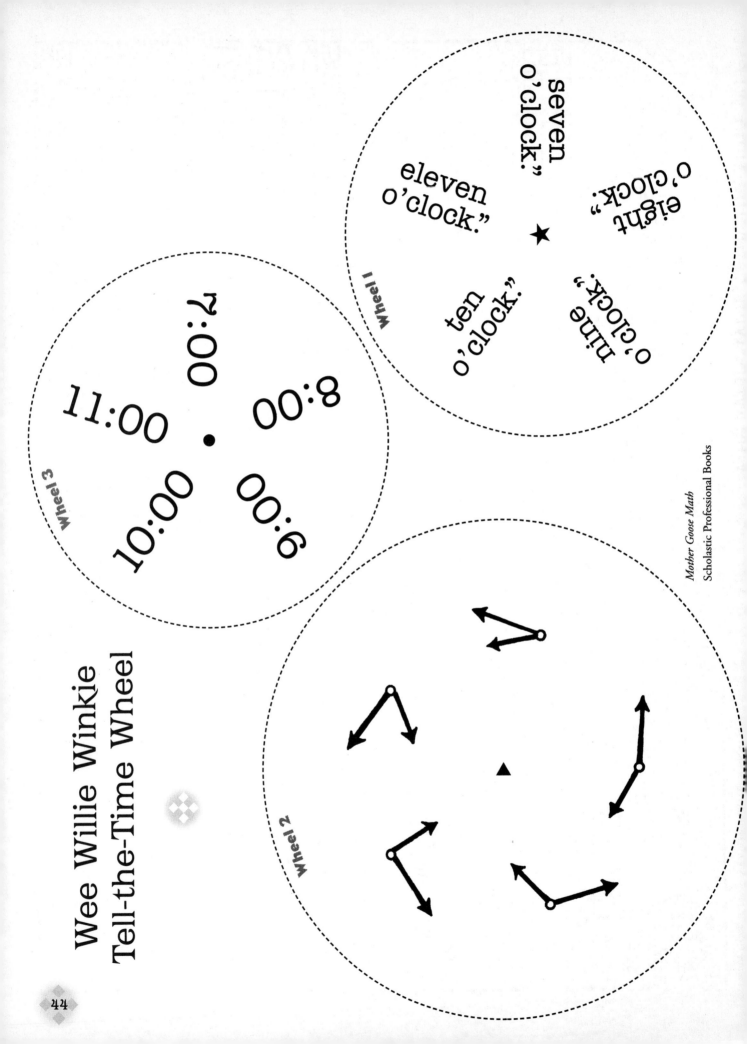

Wee Willie Winkie
Tell-the-Time Wheel

Wheel 1

seven o'clock."

eleven o'clock."

eight o'clock."

ten o'clock."

nine o'clock."

★

Wheel 2

▲

Wheel 3

7:00

8:00

9:00

10:00

11:00

•

Mother Goose Math
Scholastic Professional Books

44

Simple Simon

Simple Simon met a pieman,
Going to the fair.
Said Simple Simon to the pieman,
"Let me taste your wares."

Said the pieman to Simple Simon,
"Show me first your penny."
Said Simple Simon to the pieman,
"Indeed, I have not any."

Simple Simon

using money

★ chart paper
★ marker
★ tray
★ individual serving pies (optional)
★ several pennies, nickels, and dimes
★ self-sticking notes
★ paper plate

For each playing group:

★ pie, number cube, and coin patterns, pages 49–51
★ pocket coin pouch (see page 48) or envelope (one per child)
★ scissors
★ crayons
★ 2 sheets of construction paper
★ envelope

Getting Ready

1 Photocopy the rhyme on page 45 for each child, and write the rhyme on chart paper.

2 Place the coins on the paper plate. Then place an individual serving pie on a tray. (Or enlarge and copy one of the pie patterns on page 49, masking the price.)

3 On two sets of self-sticking notes, write the following prices: 3 cents, 5 cents, 7 cents, 15 cents, 17 cents, 20 cents. Also make just one label that says 1 cent.

4 Copy and assemble a number cube for each group. Also make copies of the pie and coin pattern pages for each group.

Reading the Rhyme

1 Read aloud the rhyme. Explain to children that wares are things that someone has to sell. In the rhyme, the wares are pies. Then ask children whether or not Simple Simon was able to buy a pie from the pieman. (*No, because he didn't have the penny needed to buy it.*)

2 Place the 1¢ sign next to the pie on the tray. Then ask two volunteers to take the roles of Simple Simon and the pieman. Give the pieman the tray to hold (and a chef hat and/or apron to wear for added fun) and give Simple Simon the plate of coins.

3 Reread the rhyme, letting Simple Simon and the pieman read their lines. When the pieman says, "Show me first your penny," ask Simple Simon to find that amount of money on the plate and use it to "buy" a pie.

4 Repeat steps 2 and 3, letting different children take the roles of Simple Simon and the pieman. Give children practice working with different combinations of coins each time by placing a different price label next to the pie and the matching label over the word *penny* in the rhyme.

✦ Buy a Pie! ✦

1 Divide the class into groups of three or four. Hand out a pie and coin pattern page to each group. Let children color and cut out the pieces. Also provide each child with a pocket coin pouch (see instructions on page 48), or an envelope for storing the coins.

2 To play, the coins are placed on a sheet of construction paper (the "bank").

3 One child in each group is the pieman. He or she displays the pies on a construction paper tray. (For added fun, let the pieman wear a chef's hat or apron.)

4 Players take turns rolling the number cube. If the player rolls "5 cents," for example, he or she takes 5 pennies or a nickel from the bank.

5 When a player has enough money, he or she can buy a pie from the pieman. Play continues until all the pies have been sold. Let children switch roles so that everyone has a chance to be the pieman.

6 To extend the activity, invite each child to count the total value of the pies he or she bought.

Mother Goose
Book Nook

✦✦✦

Benny's Pennies by Pat Brisson (Doubleday, 1993). What should Benny buy with his five new pennies? Everyone in his family wants something different! Richly textured paper collage illustrations follow Benny on his shopping expedition.

·········

My Rows and Piles of Coins by Tololwa M. Mollel (North-South Books, 1999). Set in a contemporary Tanzanian village, this charming tale follows Saruni, a young boy who saves and saves his coins in hopes of buying the bicycle of his dreams.

❖ Pocket Coin Pouch ❖

① To make each pouch, fold a square of 8-inch thin colored paper in half on the diagonal to make a triangle.

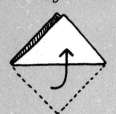

② Fold the bottom left corner up so that it touches the opposite edge of the triangle. Do the same with the bottom right corner.

③ Fold down one of the flaps at the top of the pouch. Then tuck it into the pocket on the front of the pouch.

④ Children can put their coins inside the pouch and close it by tucking the other flap inside the pocket.

More Math Fun!

Extend the activity by posing story problems for children to solve. For example:

★ Show children a pie that costs 10 cents and one that costs 5 cents. Explain that they have two dimes with which to buy these pies. How much change should the pieman give them?

★ Tell children that they have 18 cents. How many different combinations of pies could they buy? (*six: an 18-cent pie; a 3-, 5-, and 10-cent pie; a 3- and 15-cent pie; three 5-cent and one 3-cent pie; six 3-cent pies; and one 12-cent and two 3-cent pies*)

❖ Mother Goose Learning Center ❖

Coin Combos Give children practice counting larger coin amounts. Make multiple copies of the pie patterns on pages 49 and 50. Place the pie patterns, multiple sets of paper coins, glue sticks, and paper and pencils at the center. Students choose a pie, glue it to a sheet of paper, and then paste onto the paper two or three different coin combinations that equal the price of the pie.

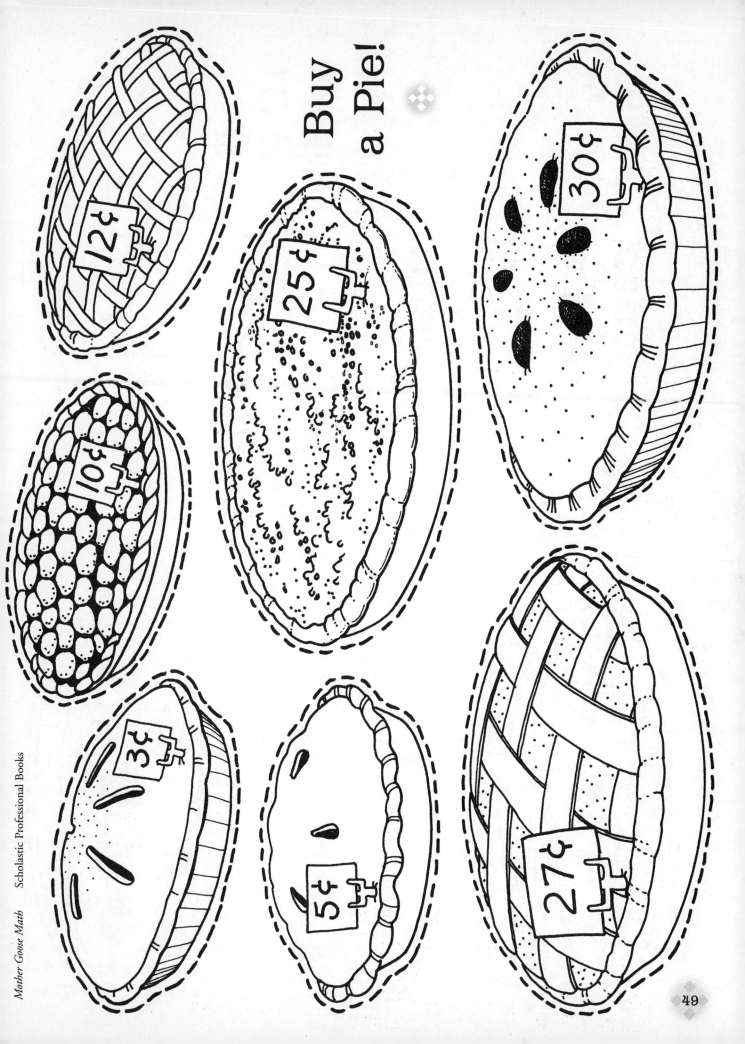

Buy a Pie!

Buy a Pie!

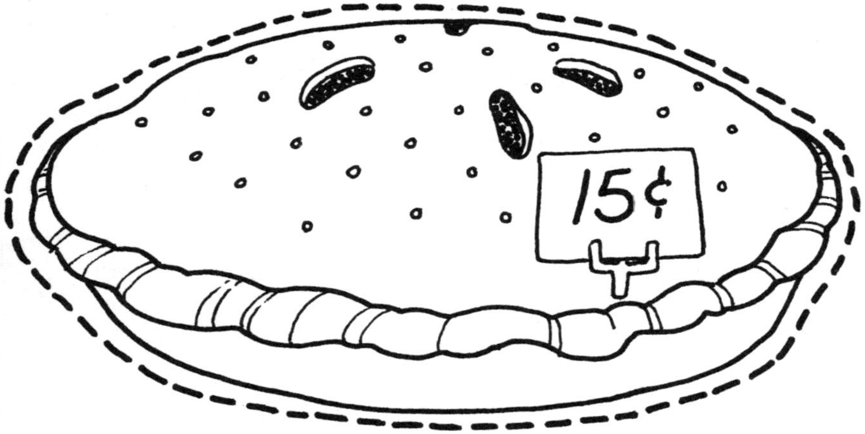

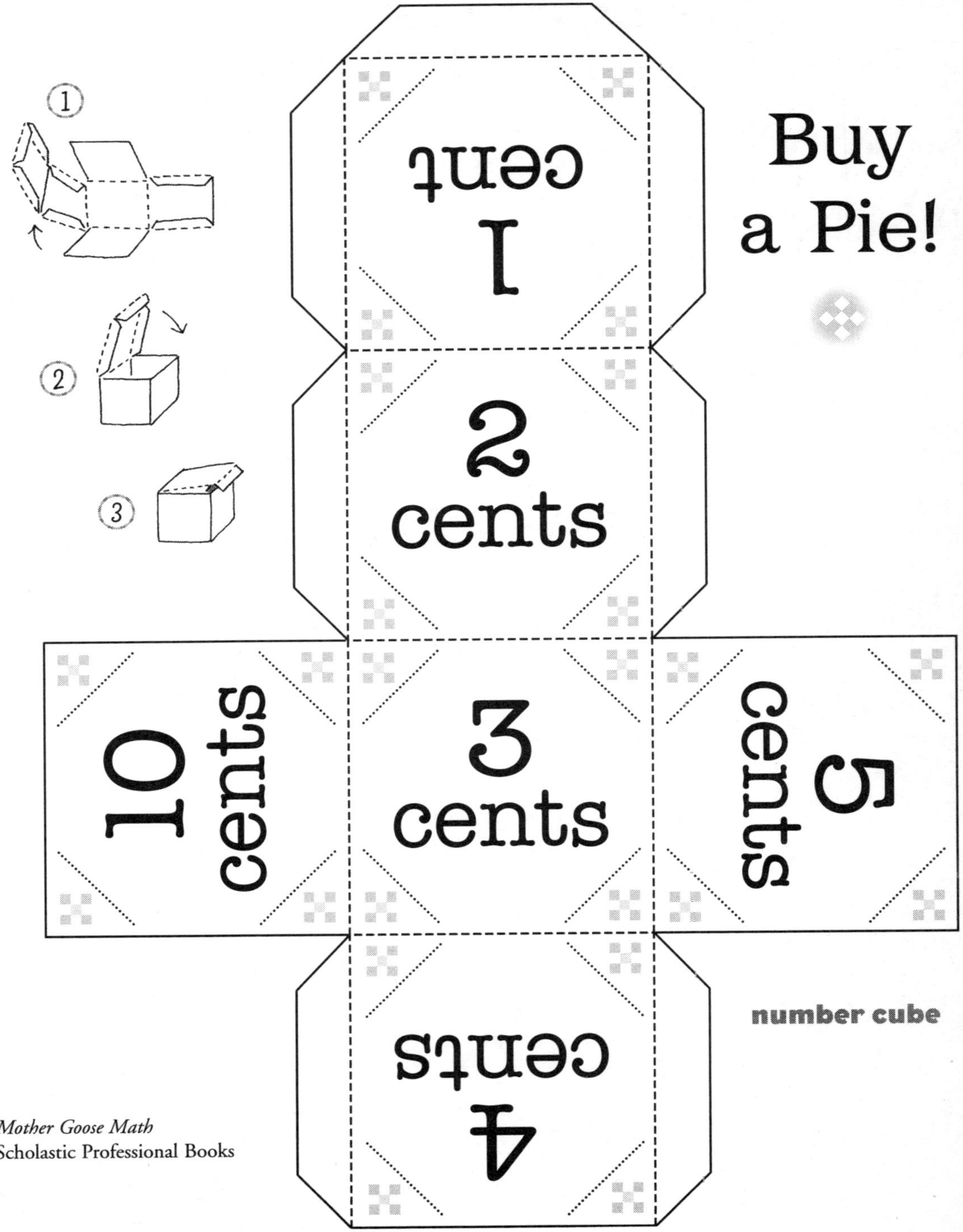

number cube

5
cents

1
cent

2
cents

3
cents

4
cents

10
cents

(1) (2) (3)

Mother Goose Math
Scholastic Professional Books

18¢

15¢

20¢

50

Buy a Pie!

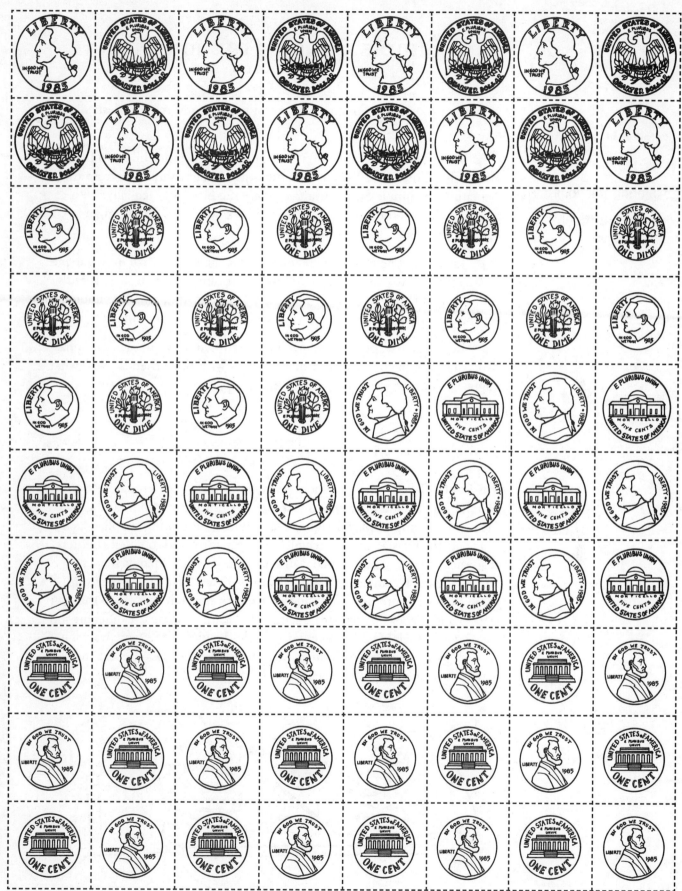

Simple Simon Fraction Pies

SKILLS

exploring fractions

identifying attributes
of shapes

MATERIALS

★ pie pattern, page 53
★ scissors
★ crayons, colored
   pencils, or markers

1 Make two copies of the pie pattern on page 53 and color as desired.

2 Invite a volunteer to be Simple Simon, and give the child two pies. Tell children that Simple Simon has just bought these pies from the pieman. Now Simple Simon wants to share the pies fairly (equally) with a friend. Invite a volunteer to be the friend. Ask children: "What might Simple Simon do?" (*give the friend one pie*)

3 Take away one pie and tell children that the pieman had only one pie left to sell to Simple Simon. How might Simple Simon share it fairly with his friend? (*He can cut the pie in half.*) Demonstrate this for children by cutting the pie pattern in half and giving one half to each of the volunteers.

4 Repeat step 3, but this time tell children that now Simple Simon has only one pie but wants to share it fairly with three friends. Now what might he do? (*cut it into four equal pieces, or quarters*)

More Math Fun!

Pie Parts To give children more practice working with simple fractions (wholes, halves, and quarters), divide the class into four groups and give each child a lump of play dough, a plastic knife, decorating supplies such as beads or dried pasta, and a piece of waxed paper to work on. Tell children that each group is going to make and decorate pies in different shapes (circle, square, rectangle, or diamond). Designate a shape for each group. Then pose story problems for children to work through, similar to those in steps 3 and 4 above. Afterward, invite each group to share the different ways they divided their pies. Did everyone divide the pies in the same way? Then let each group share their findings with the rest of the class. Repeat the activity, giving each group a chance to work with a different shape.

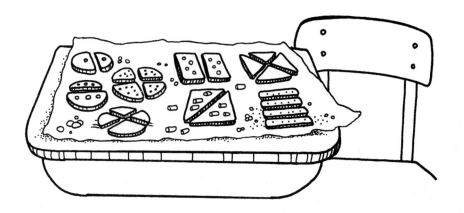

Mother Goose Learning Center

My Fraction Pie Book To help children explore equivalent fractions, make three copies of the pie pattern below. Use a ruler and a marker to draw thick lines dividing one pie in half and one pie into fourths. Leave the third pie whole. Make multiple copies of the three pages and cut out the pies. Then cut sheets of construction paper into circles measuring the same diameter as the pies. Stock a center with the pie patterns, construction paper circles, scissors, glue sticks, and a stapler. Invite children to visit the center, color the pies as desired, and then cut them apart along the solid lines. Let children use the pie parts to explore different combinations that make a whole. When they are satisfied with their arrangements, children can glue each combination onto a construction paper circle. To make a cover, have them glue a whole pie onto a construction paper circle and write "My Fraction Pie Book, by [name]." Then they can stack the circles together and staple on the left side. Encourage children to share their books with each other and to discuss the different combinations they made.

Mother Goose Book Nook

Gator Pie by Louise Mathews (Dodd, Meade, 1979). What happens when two young alligators are just about to split a pie when more and more alligators arrive, demanding their fair share, too? In this delightful introduction to fractions, children will relate to the dilemma of how to give everyone a fair share.

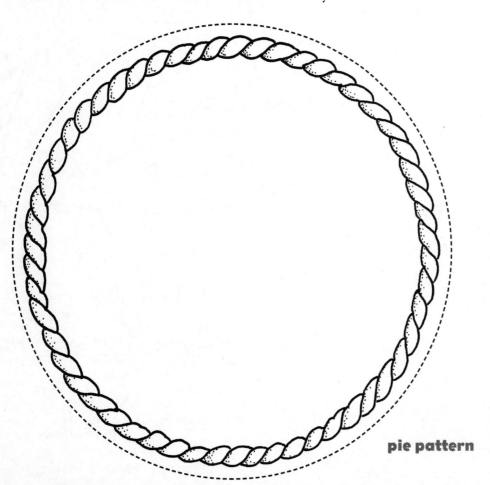

pie pattern

To Banbury Cross

Ride a cock-horse
To Banbury Cross,
To see a fine lady
Upon a white horse.
With rings on her fingers,
And bells on her toes,
She shall have music
Wherever she goes.

To Banbury Cross

Getting Ready

1 Photocopy the rhyme on page 54 for each child, and write the rhyme on chart paper. Also copy the legend on page 57 onto chart paper.

2 Make a copy of page 58 and cut out the patterns. Then follow the legend to create a sample glyph (a pictorial representation of data) to introduce to your class. (See Reading the Rhyme, below.)

3 Also make one copy of pages 57 and 58 for each child.

Reading the Rhyme

1 Read the rhyme aloud. Ask children to look at the picture on their poetry page. Then ask if they can find the cock-horse in the picture. Explain that this was a stick-toy horse played with by children long ago.

2 Ask children to look at the picture again and describe something else that they see (a lady riding a horse; she has rings on her fingers and bells on her shoe, and so on). What information do they know about this woman from the picture? (*she likes to ride horses, to dress up, to make music, and so on*)

3 Show children the glyph you prepared. Explain that a glyph is a special kind of picture that gives information about the person who made it. Point to the legend on the chart paper. Tell children that they can use the legend to find out what the glyph says about you.

4 Read aloud the legend, one element at a time, and discuss what each feature on your glyph represents. (See example, right.)

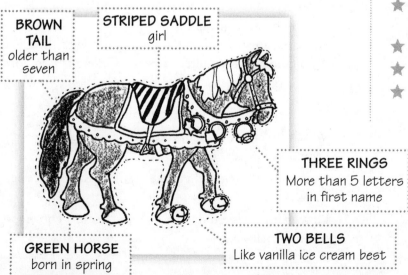

BROWN TAIL
older than seven

STRIPED SADDLE
girl

THREE RINGS
More than 5 letters in first name

TWO BELLS
Like vanilla ice cream best

GREEN HORSE
born in spring

SKILLS

collecting, organizing, and interpreting data using glyphs and graphs

MATERIALS

★ legend, page 57
★ glyph patterns, page 58
★ scissors
★ glue stick
★ crayons, colored pencils, or markers

For each child:

★ legend, page 57
★ glyph patterns, page 58
★ crayons, colored pencils, or markers
★ scissors
★ glue stick
★ sheet of construction paper

My horse is orange with a red tail.

It has a polka-dot saddle.

It has one ring around its neck.

It has four bells on its feet.

Who Am I?

❖ Banbury Cross Horse Glyph ❖

1 Tell children that they are going to create their own personal Banbury Cross horse glyphs. Give each child a copy of the legend and glyph pattern page. Review the legend with children.

2 Hand out scissors, construction paper, glue sticks, and coloring supplies. Tell children to complete one feature of their glyph at a time, and to do any coloring before cutting apart the pattern page. Then they can glue their glyph onto a sheet of construction paper.

3 Once the glyphs have been completed, divide the class into pairs to swap glyphs. What can children tell about each other based on the glyphs? Have them use the legend to find out. Then let each pair take turns sharing the information they learned with the rest of the class. Ask them to explain how they know what each feature represents.

More Math Fun!

Who Am I? Riddles Use the glyphs to pose logic problems, in the form of riddles, to sharpen students' critical thinking. (See example, left.) Then challenge children to come up with their own Who Am I? riddles to pose to each other.

Glyph Groups and Graphs Help children sort their glyphs by attributes to analyze them in another way. Divide the class into groups. Tell each group to choose one way to sort their glyphs (by the season in which they were born, their favorite flavor of ice cream, and so on). Invite each group to share its sorting method with the class.

Vary this activity by choosing six or seven of students' glyphs and sorting them into two groups. Challenge students to guess the attribute you used to group them. Guide students to look for the common attribute of all the glyphs in one of the groups.

Finally, use the floor to make a bar graph with the glyphs, using different sorting methods that children suggest. To help children interpret the graph, ask questions, such as:

⭐ How many children in the class like chocolate ice cream?

⭐ Which ice cream is the favorite of most children in the class? Least favorite? How do you know?

⭐ How many more children like [vanilla] than [strawberry]? Explain your answer.

⭐ How many children do not like ice cream? (The graph does not show this information.)

Name:

Banbury Cross
Horse Glyph
Legend

1. **Are you a boy or a girl?**

	boy	girl
Pattern on Saddle		

2. **In what season were you born?**

	winter	spring	summer	fall
Color of Horse	**white**	**green**	**blue**	**orange**

3. **How old are you?**

	five years old	six years old	seven years old	older than seven
Color of Tail	**yellow**	**red**	**black**	**brown**

4. **How many letters are in your first name?**

	fewer than five	exactly five	more than five
Number of Rings Around Neck	**1**	**2**	**3**

5. **What ice cream flavor do you like best?**

	chocolate	vanilla	strawberry	another flavor
Number of Bells on Feet	**1**	**2**	**3**	**4**

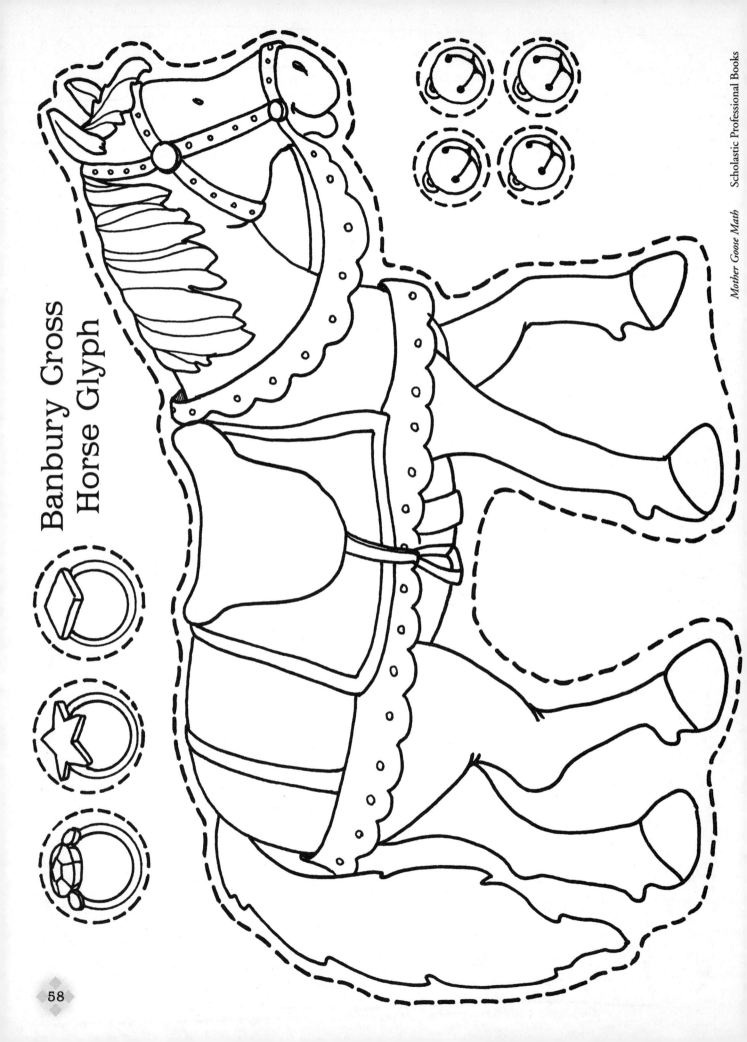

Banbury Cross
Horse Glyph

Mother Goose Math   Scholastic Professional Books

Mrs. Hen

Chook, chook, chook, chook, chook,
Good morning, Mrs. Hen.
How many chicks have you got?
Madam, I've got ten.
Four of them are yellow,
And four of them are brown,
And two of them are speckled,
The nicest in the town.

Mrs. Hen

SKILLS

sorting and classifying by attributes using decision trees and Venn diagrams

MATERIALS

★ chart paper
★ marker
★ chick patterns, page 64
★ scissors
★ crayons or markers
★ tape

For each student pair:

★ henhouse game board, pages 62–63
★ chick patterns, page 64
★ yellow and brown crayons

Getting Ready

1 Make a copy of the rhyme on page 59 for each child, and write the rhyme on chart paper.

2 Make one copy of the chick finger-puppet pattern page for each child. Have children color four of the chicks yellow and four of them brown, leaving two chicks with speckles uncolored, and cut them out. (There will be two leftover speckled chicks.) Help tape each puppet to fit on children's fingers.

3 Make an additional copy of the chick pattern page and the two halves of the game board for each pair of students. Tape together the halves of the board. These materials will be used in Chick and Nest Match-Up, page 61.

Reading the Rhyme

1 Read the rhyme aloud. Ask children to name the different kinds of chicks described in the rhyme. How many of each kind does Mrs. Hen have? How many chicks are there in all?

2 Invite children to read the rhyme with you. Ask them to keep their hands in their laps until the chicks are mentioned. Then tell them to make each group of chicks appear and scurry around (wiggle their fingers in the air) until all ten chicks have appeared. Repeat this process several times.

3 Read the fifth, sixth, and seventh lines of the rhyme in reverse order and let children make the correct groups of chicks appear.

Chick and Nest Match-Up

1 Give each pair of children a copy of the chick pattern page. (For this activity, children will not be using the chicks as finger puppets.) Have each pair color eight of the chicks with the characteristics listed at right and then cut them out. (They will have four chicks left over.)

2 Ask children to describe some of the attributes of their chicks. On the chalkboard, list their responses (standing, sitting, brown, brown with speckles, and so on).

3 Hand out a copy of the henhouse game board to each student pair. Tell children to pick any four chicks each. Then explain that the chicks need their help in returning to their own nests in the henhouse.

4 To play, each player puts a chick on START. The first player moves a chick along the paths to a nest. When a chick reaches a fork in the path, the player chooses the direction to follow according to the chick's attributes. For example, if a player has a standing brown chick, the chick moves to the left at the first fork, then left at the second fork, and right at the third fork to reach the correct nest. Then the second player takes a turn guiding a chick to its nest.

5 The game is over when both players get all of their chicks safely tucked in their nests.

- one standing brown chick
- one sitting brown chick
- one standing brown speckled chick
- one sitting brown speckled chick
- one standing yellow chick
- one sitting yellow chick
- one standing yellow speckled chick
- one sitting yellow speckled chick

More Math Fun!

Chick Sort! Provide each pair of children with a large sheet of construction paper on which you've drawn two overlapping 6-inch circles (a Venn diagram). Using the chicks from the above activity, ask one child in each pair to use the circles to sort the chicks into two groups so that the chicks in each group are alike in some way (for example, speckled chicks and yellow chicks). The partner then tries to guess the attributes used to sort them. After each child has had several opportunities to sort the chicks into two groups, challenge children to use the overlapping circle as well, sorting the chicks into three groups (for example, chicks that are yellow and speckled). What happens to the chicks that belong to none of the groups? (*They go outside the circles.*)

Mother Goose Book Nook

Billy's Button by William Accordsi (Greenwillow, 1992). As they turn the pages of this book, young readers will have lots of fun trying to find Billy's button among an assortment of buttons with different attributes. Look for this intriguing title in your library or a used-book store.

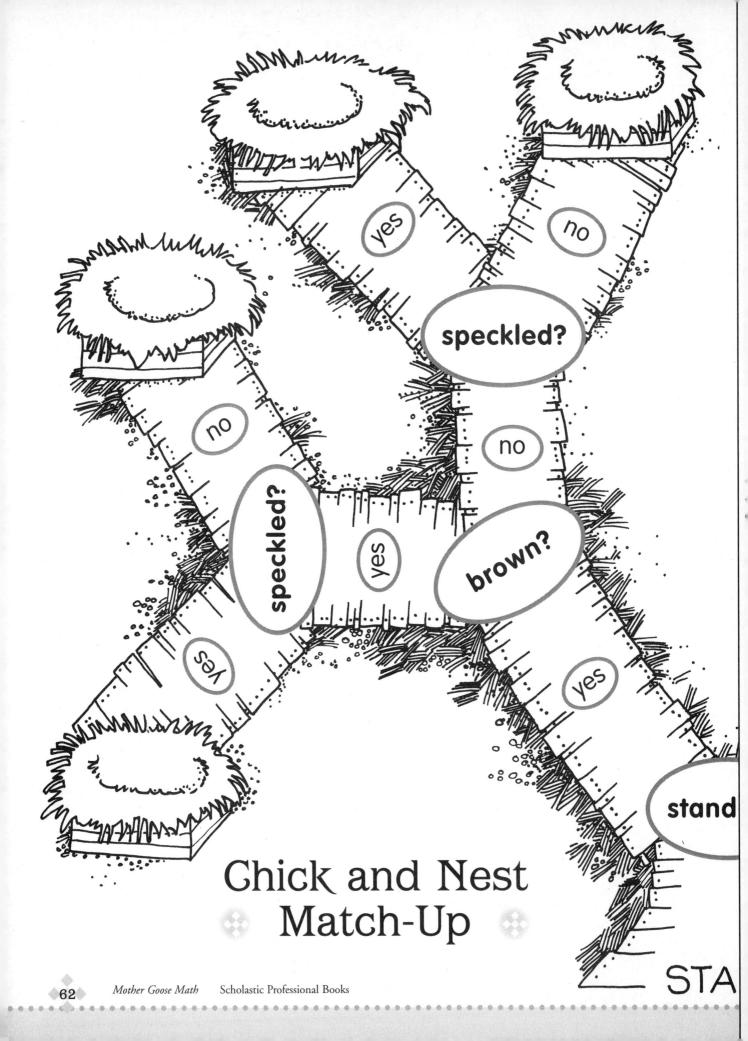

Chick and Nest Match-Up

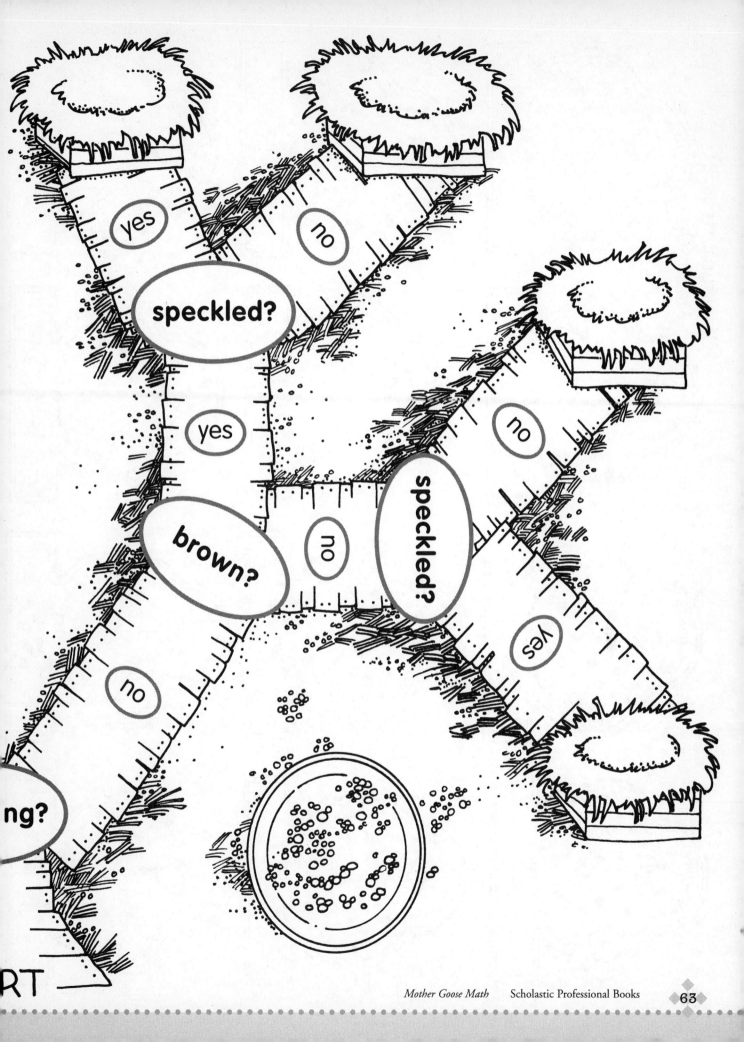

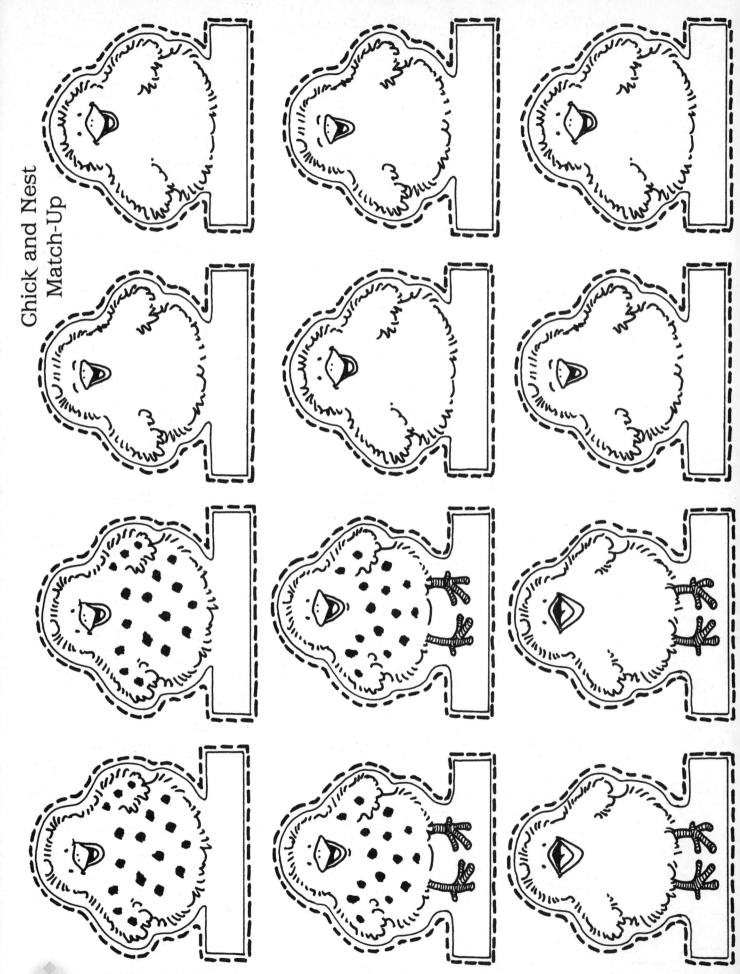

Chick and Nest Match-Up

Mother Goose Math   Scholastic Professional Books